SENSE OF TIME

SENSE OF TIME

Poetry

Richard Wiener

Copyright © 2010 by Richard Wiener.

Library of Congress Control Number:		2009913205
ISBN:	Hardcover	978-1-4500-1147-1
	Softcover	978-1-4500-1146-4
	Ebook	978-1-4500-1148-8

All rights reserved. No part of this book may be reproduced or transmitted in any form or by any means, electronic or mechanical, including photocopying, recording, or by any information storage and retrieval system, without permission in writing from the copyright owner.

This book was printed in the United States of America.

To order additional copies of this book, contact:
Xlibris Corporation
1-888-795-4274
www.Xlibris.com
Orders@Xlibris.com
71480

CONTENTS

PREFACE 9
POE-*esy* (1951) 11
THE MUSICIAN (1952) 12
SUNSET REFLECTION (1954) 14
NEUROTIC (1956) 15
ON BEING TAKEN TOO SERIOUSLY (1956) 16
LONGING—I (1956) 17
LONGING—II (1956) 18
LONGING—III (1956) 19
LONGING—IV (1956) 20
AT THE DEATH OF A FRIEND (1957) 21
ODE TO OLIVETTI (1960) 22
PAIN OF NOSTALGIA (1960) 23
JFK—IN MEMORIAM (November 23, 1963) 24
TRANSITIONS (1970) 25
IN SILENCE (1971) 26
RISE AND FALL (1971) 27
NEWS ITEM (1980) 28
PERPETUAL MOTION (1984) 29
SISYPHUS (1984) 30
DEPRESSION (1985) 32
THOUGHTS ON AWAKENING (1988) 33
WALL POSTER (1988) 34
AFTER ALL THE LAMENTATIONS (1988) 35

BECOMING (1988)	36
SHIFTING LIVES (1988)	37
KRISTALLNACHT (1988)	38
HOME FOR SALE (1989)	40
PROUST'S LABORS LOST (1991)	42
HOMAGE TO AURELIUS (1991)	43
HISTORY (1993)	44
FRANCINE IS DEAD (1993)	46
FROM THE EDGE OF THE GRAVE (1994)	48
AUTUMN REFLECTION (1994)	49
PAST BOUNDARIES (1994)	50
TRANSPORT (1996)	51
RENUNCIATION (1997)	53
A POEM FROM DAD (2000)	54
PRISONERS ALL (2000)	55
VOYAGE (2001)	56
THE PASSING SCENE (2002)	58
HOMAGE TO ANAGNOS (2002)	59
RETURNING TO PORT (2002)	60
TURNING CORNERS (2002)	62
CURRIED SHRIMP (2004)	63
DESPAIR (2005)	64
TRACES (2005)	65
RETICENCE (February 2007)	66
WHAT FATHERS BEAR (2007)	67
THE DARK STAIR (2008)	68
AFTERWARDS (2002)	69

For my children and grandchildren

PREFACE

I have waited most of my life to take the plunge, and here, for better or worse, am hurling my poetry out into the world. It seems that I have finally accepted the reality that I do not have unlimited time to wait.

These fifty poems may be regarded as a survey of work written over the span of half a century. The earliest poem *(Poe-esy)* derives from my graduate student days at Princeton. While some of the poems written during the succeeding decade manifest the insouciance of youth, and lack the gravitas of my later work, I have included them specifically to illustrate the theme of this collection: the changes that time brings. Other poems deal with specific life events: the Holocaust *(Kristallnacht)*, bereavement *(At the Death of a Friend, JFK—in Memoriam, Francine is Dead),* divorce *(Home for Sale).* Several of the later poems (*Traces, Renunciation, After all the Lamentations, Afterwards)* are part of the *Seasons of Men's Lives* workshop which is presented every five years in my men's community, *The ManKind Project.*

Because, in recent years, I have enjoyed the pleasure of mentoring men of diverse ages, I am constantly reminded of what it was like to be young, middle aged and young old, and this theme—the flow of life—has informed my work.

POE-*esy* (1951)

Emerging from the cloistered hall, I paused.
I gasped. I thought: but this is Elsinore.
Where else have shadows fallen on a nightly stair
So terrifying, so frantic, and bizarre?
Look how the luminous lamp doth in the courtyard glow,
Scatt'ring the barren tree shades round the hill,
Tilting the landscape's horrid unreality
To frighten lonely wanderers abroad.
Where else have through the paneling of a pane
(A clouded, shrouded pane set in the casement wall),
The eerie, whining sounds of some odd, mournful thing
Issued more dolefully?
The very night's afloat upon some deep,
And dreams my only raft till I awake.

THE MUSICIAN (1952)

A minstrel, fleeing from the rain, and from himself,
Stepped down into a casement, into solitude,
When, through a door, alone and haunting,
Sang a violin, as if to him; and he, without a thought,
He turned the knob, and stepped inside.

Close by the door he stood, alone and dripping rain
Upon the shimmering carpet. Only ears
Had he, not even eyes, for oh, he dared not
Look over there to see who it could be
That played to him alone, a love song to a minstrel.

It rose and rose, like vaunting Pegasus,
Then hummed a bit, and rose again,
So warm and halting, like an ardent lover
Upon his first confession, shy at first, and then,
Caught by the magic of it, leaping on and on
To foolish, aching protestation.

How long he stood there, no one knows.
At least he did not hear the rain that puckered on the pane.
At least he did not hear the ticking of the clock, until it struck,
Boom! His hands flew startled to his brow.
Boom! He woke, and raised his limpid eyes
To meet those of the player, who stared
Enraged across the room at him.

An ugly man, quite bald,
And bearing in his eyes the malice
Of all the outcasts of the world.
His eyes aflame, he lunged across the room,
To claw with those same hands that lately drew

Such poignant fancies from his violin,
Into the minstrel's threadbare shoulders.
Berserk, the latter fled into the street,
Into the dark and loveless street, and back
Into his frightened, groping self.

SUNSET REFLECTION (1954)

So still the land, so still the sea
That after lo, these many years
My heart is quite alone with me
As summer dies and evening nears.

How many ships have I not sailed,
How many shores not walked upon.
Whenever love and friendship failed,
'T was to the sea that I was drawn.

I gave my heart to you, o waves,
And to the strand my sullen pride.
I found the solitude that saves
Upon the bosom of the tide.

And now I'm home. The brackish sea
Floods back into my consciousness.
The endless vistas comfort me.
The barren wind is my caress.

And when my time has come at last
I shall not grieve from man to part
If from a ship I maybe cast
Into the sea that knows my heart.

NEUROTIC (1956)

You are afraid of being an illusion,
Of being loved for talents not your own.
You dread the consequences of confusion,
And won't feel safe until the truth be known.

What is this truth you wish to make explicit?
What craven secrets must you bring to light?
Perhaps your dreams appear to you illicit,
Perhaps you are a creature of the night.

Or else you're troubled by hallucinations,
Or drink in secret, take hashish or dope.
Perhaps your list of weird preoccupations
Includes such things as incest, snakes, or rope.

Which of these lunacies forms your attraction?
Is it your superego or your id?
I hope this truth will give you satisfaction:
It's all of them, you crazy mixed up kid.

ON BEING TAKEN TOO SERIOUSLY (1956)

Whatever I have said or done
Since we two met,
Whatever foolishness or fun,
Whatever laughter, sadness, hope—
They're due to you, you silly dope.

If I'm morose, sarcastic, coy,
That's my regret,
And yet, whatever real joy
I feel, you mustn't ridicule,
For it's all due to you, you fool.

At times I tend to be a bore,
Or, sadder yet,
I may talk too much of *amor*.
But when my spirits seem to droop,
It's all your fault, you nincompoop.

LONGING—I (1956)

Tonight you're coming (so, at least, you said)
To spend an hour or two with me, to throw
A few brief bits of happiness my way,
To hold me tight, until it's time to go.
You have no time, I fully understand
That it's a sacrifice for you to come at all.
Another waits, you would be missed at home,

And even now it's late. You'd better call.
The telephone is in the other room.
But close the door; I could not bear that tone
With someone else, someone whose heart must ache
As much as mine at being left alone.

One day I'll leave off waiting in the rain
And find the heart to say: don't come again.

LONGING—II (1956)

Another hour gone. It's ten past ten,
And still dead silence from the telephone.
I put aside my book, lay down my pen,
And feel—oh God—so empty and alone.
I know I shall not sleep, but also know
That waiting leads to nothing but despair.
Perhaps there's something on the radio
To make this heartache easier to bear.
The hours tick by. The years tick by. I wait
And brew myself another cup of tea.
I can't decide whether to love or hate,
And tell myself at last to wait and see.

LONGING—III (1956)

A night of waiting turns the heart
From hope to grief to bitterness,
And mute resentments well may start
From longings for a dear caress.

What right have you to cause me pain?
You do not know (nor would you care)
That love, were it to come again
Could plunge me deep into despair.

Although you did not say you'd call,
I waited, waited endlessly
For every footstep in the hall,
And fell asleep, in tears, at three.

LONGING—IV (1956)

You bring them back, all the forgotten years:
The moon across the dark, cavernous valley,
Limning the trees, startling the soul.
The lonely beach at night, the fire
Shivering in the wind.
And all the dreams, songs, sighs
Belonging to those years.

Where have you come from, and why have you come?
My heart's too old for you, too weary, too inured
To solitude. I asked for nothing, yet you gave,
And I accepted.
I warn you, don't rouse appetites you cannot still,
Or I shall hate you.

AT THE DEATH OF A FRIEND (1957)

Last night you lived, today you are no more.
Your heart no longer beats, that weary heart,
So burdened holding back the flood of life
That finally it had to break apart.

I mourn your early death, yet even more
I mourn the interrupted flow of love
That only now promised to find its way
To you, into that lonely, barren grove
Where you had hid so long. What happiness
Love could have given you, what hope, what years!
Your longings would have eased, you would have seen
The ecstasies of heaven through your tears.

And now it's over. All these dusty words
Can't change the bitter verdict of the gods.

ODE TO OLIVETTI (1960)

The New World owes the Old World much.
There hands have never lost their touch.
And when it comes to touch control,
Whom is it one and all extol?
Whom else but Olivetti.

Here's beauty harnessed for the beast.
She gives the most, and he the least.
And who provides the proper spacing
To send the bestial pulses racing?
Who else but Olivetti.

She croons romantically on key,
And leaves his fingers rather free.
He smiles, hands on her tabulator:
"All clear. I'm set to grab you later."
How sweet, with Olivetti.

Of myriad lovely things—Italian
She most deserves a gold medallion.
She's better than spaghetti,
Or plays by Ugo Betti.
She's none but . . . Olivetti

PAIN OF NOSTALGIA (1960)

The months of my life's spring and summer pass
Without the kiss of bees upon the rose.
I lie, no more expectant, in the grass
And contemplate the season as it goes.
As yet, the leaves stir softly 'gainst the sky,
The wildflowers curtsy gently in the wind,
A brace of fawn-flecked pheasants flutter by,
To vanish out of sight, and out of mind.

So many brilliant images forgot,
So many sounds, scents, sighs beyond recall.
Rememb'ring childhood summers, do I not
Prefer to guard the present by a wall
Of ill-feigned ennui and lethargy
To keep jealous remembrances at bay?

And when the old bells chime, do I not flee,
Stopping my ears against the music's sway?
The fire is not out, its heat remains.
Upon the flagstones, its reflections dart.
Forgetting has its place, but there are stains
Etchéd indelibly upon the aging heart.
So many years have worn their message there.
The clock is broke, I fear, beyond repair.

JFK—IN MEMORIAM (November 23, 1963)

He was a man, recall, only a man,
And yet he sipped the nectar of the gods,
Rose in his stirrups, kind, brave,
Spurning all limits.

Oh, others try, learn lessons,
Rehearse stances, write what they ought
On history's page.
But he: 't was never ought with him,
Always felt, quickened, bright.

Weep not for him, secure now,
But for us, all, all bereaved
As of a Pericles. A golden age
Is gone. When
Will come such another?

TRANSITIONS (1970)

A single man walks down the empty street.
His footsteps echo, ring, die down.
A cat mews in a doorway, blinking.

Around the corner stands another man,
Biting his lip, scanning the headlines.
Off in the distance someone flies a kite.

What has become of red-haired Willy Hogan,
Of Mary Jane, and Bonzo, our great dane?
Where have they gone, the golden courtyard hours
Without an end?

They all live somewhere, somewhere else than I do.
Maybe in villas, or in railroad flats.
Someone said Willy joined, I think it was the navy,
Learned electronics or some stuff like that.

And Mary Jane no doubt has several children,
Lives out in Teaneck, drinks, and dyes her hair.
On Tuesdays, she plays tennis with her neighbor,
And on off-nights she plays at solitaire.

There's old Louisa leaning out her window.
Imagine, every Sunday of her life
Never to have a body in for tea.

IN SILENCE (1971)

A swan glides in the distance
Across the shallow pond
Aware and proud.

A tulip blooms at dawn,
Red cup tilting in praise
Strong yet temporal.

A brook rushes o'er boulders
Down, down to the meadow
Where mute cows graze.

These ask no questions
That is their worth
Do not claw half-healed wounds
That is their discretion.

We need their silence, resignation
To be, simply be
While we, the knowing
Seek always to become.

We too need but to glide
Across the shallow pond of life
Aware but humble, to bloom
In the morning of our years
Without resenting our mortality
To tumble ceaselessly
Down over shoals of sorrow
To that final meadow.

RISE AND FALL (1971)

Falling and falling and falling and falling,
Raindrops and snowflakes and blossoms and hail,
All things returning to earth have their rhythm,
Rising ecstatically, plunging.
                                          They fail,
Those who count only lumens of sunlight,
Fleeing the downpour, dreading the winter,
Wishing that things would forever fly upward—
Fail, in the end, to consider desire:
Mankind for manna, starlings for rain worms,
Roses for showers, grasses for dew.
Let us rejoice, then, both in the rising,
Climbing the long stair of earthly endeavor,
And in the prospect that lies down below us,
Lightening burdens, cool evening air.

NEWS ITEM (1980)

The Senator from Maine writes poetry,
And earns 5K a year on it,
With undisguised satisfaction.

The Senator from Arkansas writes prose,
Although of undistinguished kind,
To which he owes his reelection.

How nice that bodybuilders paint,
That Miss America plays the harp
And shy housewives do modern dance.

Continuous as the stars that shine
America is a chorus line
Along the shores of Sheepshead Bay.

And where the flying fishes play,
The mermaids, singing each to each
Have eaten everyone, hurray!

PERPETUAL MOTION (1984)

The force goes forward, or it dies.
There is no middle ground. A slow
Deceleration bears the seed
Of ultimate decay, as life's
Momentum ebbs, and entropy
Draws downward all that does not rise.

Where does it lead, the dance of life,
The pulsing, rocking, whirligig?
The dancers, flushed and feverish,
Have barely entered from the wings,
Done a few turns, a waltz or two,
Enamored of the music's lilt,
And then moved breathlessly
To shadowed rooms, lost to our view,
While other dancers take their place.

There is no ending, so it seems,
To this perpetual motion, no,
No interruption, save for quick
Refreshments in the intervals.
The faces change, the partners, too,
But it, the dance of life, goes on
Perpetually.

SISYPHUS (1984)

Man is constrained to move things.
The child plays marbles, rolls a hoop,
Delights in tossing balls and discs
That float so easily through space.

The youth is made of sterner stuff.
He puts the shot, throws javelins
And discus, wrestles comrades to the ground,
Delighting in ungirded strength
That still seems boundless.

Unnoticed, things grow heavier.
Year upon year, the gold of youth
Turns, first to silver,
Then copper, and then lead,
And things hurled radiantly through space
Turn into boulders, massive, and inert.

And yet, man is constrained to move them,
Through verdant plain, up the faint rise
That leads into the dark'ning wood,
Then up a steep and daunting mountainside
That looms incredibly above.
                                          At first
He sings his way, believing it the mere
Continuation of his childhood play,
But as he goes, his songs grow soft,
Then silent. All his might is now
Barely sufficient for the task.

The seasons pass, the sun grows hot,
Then hides behind the summit. Yet he strives,
And manages at last, to reach the height.
He stops, scarcely believing that his work
Is now complete, sits on a rock
And contemplates the view.

Alas, beyond his ken, the boulder moves,
Loosed from its mooring slides,
Toward the precipice, so late attained,
Gathers momentum, hurtles down,
Down to the valley, whence it came.

Man stands aghast, first disbelieving,
Then stricken. All his life, his labor,
Gone for nought. Seized by despair,
He buries face in hands and sits
Distraught upon his rock.

The sun has fled, on distant summits
Sit dark'ning clouds. A storm's about to burst.
A streak of lightning, rolls of thunder, then
The rain, drops first, now torrents,
Drenching him, flaying him where he sits
Mourning what's lost.

DEPRESSION (1985)

Rememb'ring the intensity of pain,
The numbing of desire, and the loss
Of friends, I hid my face, and all alone
Ran secretly from niche to vestibule,
Dodging all eyes, denying every want,
And seeking, always seeking, without goal.

The barren woods, engirdled by a fog
Of specters, seemed like sanctuary enough,
But left me windswept, desolate, and chilled.
The world moved on, my generation came
Of age, jumped in and seized the waiting reins,
While I, still staring, stricken, and aghast
Down corridors of vanished time, but froze
In place.
        What is it now for this dead soul
To leap to sudden life, to celebrate
The feast without beginning, without end,
To drown in wanton wine mingled with tears,
To laugh, exulting even in man's fate,
To know that death in life is worse than any death?

THOUGHTS ON AWAKENING (1988)

How curious that not till morning light
Our spectral thoughts conspire to do their worst,
That after sleeping soundly through the night
We greet the dawn in gloomy thoughts immersed.

Dread intimations of mortality
Feint boldly then against our unmasked face,
Remembered loss of love, the freighted past,
The childhood exile from a rooted place.

We set dire fantasies adrift beyond recall
By the unguarded, still half-slumb'ring mind
Deprived of reason. Random thoughts uncoil,
Apocalyptic visions strike us blind.

The minute hand moves on. At last resolve
To shuffle off the labyrinthine pall
Thrusts us upright. We contemplate the day,
One more. We are still here, and still alive.

WALL POSTER (1988)

At the Odeon Casino,
Circa nineteen-twenty-five,
Reigns an *aria misteriosa*,
Muted moments come alive.

In this near-surreal fancy
Romance seems so debonair:
His ironic, vain monocle,
Her plumed cloche, his *savoir faire*.

Her bejeweled hand, the pallor
Of her arms, her back, her face,
Her world-weary eyes in shadow
Gazing somewhere into space.

As he guides her through the ballroom
How her frock flares out behind.
They are dancing like two strangers,
Yet they linger in the mind.

AFTER ALL THE LAMENTATIONS (1988)

After all the lamentations,
Withered leaves across the hearth,
Mildewed mem'ries dying slowly,
Fading, fading, nothing worth.

Was that moment once the present,
Did we touch and breathe that air,
Breast the surf, run nude together
On that far, fantastic shore?

In that photo, you are smiling,
Reckless of the thief of time,
And those roses spell forever
Paris, nineteen-sixty-nine.

Love—or was it lust?—remembered,
Was it real? Is it now?
After all the lamentations
It's impossible to know.

BECOMING (1988)

My path is littered with discarded selves,
Each terrified to die, clinging to life
With frantic desperation, just as though
It had the right to persevere, whereas
It choked and hindered the emerging self
That struggled to be born.
                              It is no sin
To kill and kill again what holds us captive,
To bear and bear again successive progeny
That replicates (not quite) what came before,
Vesting what was inchoate,
Risking what was secure.

And who shall know this novel stranger I?
He is a relative, reminiscent in glance,
Gesture and voice of him so lately dead,
Unmourned, remembered faintly, if at all,
And buried none too soon.

SHIFTING LIVES (1988)

When other lives diverge from mine,
When friends are relocated in Vermont,
An aunt and uncle separate, or else
An old classmate retires, I feel a chill,
A perilous *frisson*.
                        The world does pass
So quickly, and the past does telescope
Our mem'ries into fading photographs.

My best friend feels his age. His smile
Is cordial still, yet wary, round the mouth,
Of coming seasons round the bend.
His premiums grow steep, his hair recedes,
The very passion oozes from his bones,
Yet he survives, for now, till next we meet I hope.

An aging partner, working on his roof,
Loses his footing, drops twelve feet
Onto a concrete slab, and stays in traction
For a month or two. He will not be the same
When he returns to work, he will not be the same
Ever again.

The human landscape shifts,
But I walk on, accepting losses, hoping to recoup,
Yet noting that the odds favor the house.

KRISTALLNACHT (1988)

A burst of shattering glass
A brick comes hurtling through the window
Fronting the street, a quiet thoroughfare
But now, tonight, seething with people,
People we know, neighbors, surging
Like angry waves, bearing torches,
Screaming up at the windows, threatening
The utterly defenseless, frightened Jews.

The search for weapons ended, he strides for the door,
My mother clinging to him for dear life.
"Oh please, I beg you, please don't open . . ."
He shakes her off, the door flies on its hinges
And they burst in, a dozen of them, men we know—
The baker's son, the boy who brings the milk,
The representatives of ordinary life
In this small town. They are in civvies,
To be sure, like paid-off partisans.

"Ihr Judenschweine!" yells the first,
Swinging his axe aloft in reckless circles,
Herding the wide-eyed, trembling victims
Into the corridor, against the wall.
"We're going to kill you all," shouts one,
And spits. The torches flicker just above our heads.
And then we hear the crash, the first of many,
As tables, cupboards, cabinets, and chairs,
Beds, desks, and china closets are smashed to smithereens.

With "Blood and Honor" knives they slash
The mattresses, upholstery, clothes ripped from closets.
Fine crystal strewn in myriad shards,
The heirloom china, cups by Rosenthal,
The very sum and substance of material lives
Lies here in ruins.

Are we next? The social contract
That men take for granted, a dead letter now,
We're at the mercy of men's basest instincts,
And who can save us? Will we all be murdered?
Will this incomprehensible insanity
Find issue in the shedding of our blood?
"We're going to kill you all," they'd said.
Was that a vow? For when—tonight? Right now?

After an hour or two that, to a child,
Seemed an eternity, a never-ending nightmare,
The beasts, sated with blood, file out,
Less vocal now, ashamed perhaps of where their lust
Has carried them. The sounds subside,
A deadly silence falls, we are struck dumb,
Stare hollow-eyed at one another, transmuted
Forever.

HOME FOR SALE (1989)

"Spring's the best time to sell," the agent said.
"Azaleas make a difference, mark my word."
It's May, and she is showing them my house
(Our house, we used to call it). Even now
Its slopes and angles speak to me, remind
Of Sunday brunches with the *New York Times*,
Grilled grapefruit, mocha coffee, and croissants,
The deck dappled with sunlight, and the vine
Twisting and twisting, pulling the wire mesh,
So carefully attached, from its mooring.

We think to save ourselves from chaos by four walls,
By rugs and curtains, chests, and wicker chairs,
Mere items bought in shops, arranged with taste,
And lived with for a time. What permanence
Is possible with uttermost control?
What fiat, what imprimatur assures
That what we grow attached to, will remain?

The music, oh, duets she and I played,
Flute and piano, Brahms if mem'ry serves,
A shared glass of *Mateus* 'mid the scores,
And harmony reigned one fleeting hour.
                                                            I see
They're coming through. The wife is smiling, while
The agent says, "They like it. Do you think
You'd knock a few bucks off for a quick sale?"
Roses of Sharon in the driveway, and the hoop
Where we shot baskets when my boy was young.
Too little room for dribbling in that yard,
Especially with the club house I put up
For them to host their friends in sleeping bags.
Oh, what the hell.
"Let's talk about it. Sure."
This is not *au revoir*, my house (our house),
This is good-bye.

PROUST'S LABORS LOST (1991)

The past revisited: of what avail
Is it to sift through ashes of our youth,
To rummage through the catalogue of years
Best left forgotten, lest the ancient pain
Emerge revivified? "Time heals all wounds,"
They say, but does it? Are there not events
Buried alive, that mold'ring lie, interred
So deep, so seemingly secure, that yet
Retain their power to impact on our lives?

And what of loves, of lusts that beckoned us
To unpremeditated cruelties,
Depravities uncountenanced today
By our present, better selves, informed
By time and untoward events? What use
To ride in vain pursuit of truths unknown,
Perchance unknowable? We think to trace
The source of our late predicaments,
But landscapes alter, wellsprings desiccate.
The past revisited is not the past
Recaptured. That remains, at last, enigma.

HOMAGE TO AURELIUS (1991)

Why be astonished at the change time brings
As if the circumstances of our birth
Were more than happenstance, a snapshot
Of but one moment in our brief sojourn,
Our evanescent presence on this earth?
The singers, players, runners of our youth
Fade from the limelight, lose their voices, slow
Their pace, are lost from sight, to be replaced
By others. Nothing lasts more than an instant.
We build memorials, seek, in vain,
To husband meaning, keep alive the past.
To no avail. The Coliseum cracks,
The clavichord's archaic in our time,
And what know we of serfdom? Scholars try
To draw historic parallels, to summon
Modern allusions, but the past,
Well-draped, yields but a wraith,
Not flesh and blood, not what our forbears felt,
What they imagined, how they saw their world.
Ponder how many madeleines we will,
All our endeavors come at last to naught.

HISTORY (1993)

The history of man is more than dates,
The reigns of kings, the tales of battles lost and won,
The dark imprimatur of evil upon a supine race.
It is the slow, inexorable crawl out of the mire of subjugation,
Of meek obeisance, to freedom.
The longer the oppression, the bloodier the thrust.

Throughout our world, seeking rebirth,
We still see raw scars of tyranny,
The fruits of late humiliations
Inflicted on those enslaved for centuries,
And now, at last, claiming their own.
It is no wonder their resentments, long hidden,
Burst forth in ugly ways:
Brother kills brother, rapes his widow, mutilates his sons.

How many generations will it take for rages to be spent,
For men to recognize their mutual need?
Who can extract the venom accumulated over eons,
And is there time for that?

The history of each of us, as well, is the slow sum
Of many an event, reaction, act of love and hate.
To understand another is as difficult
As to understand the history of France,
Perhaps more difficult.
Yes, we presume to know, we say we understand, but can we?
All we can do is generalize, project and empathize.

Remembering the stages of my life,
How many attitudes have I not struck, changing from child to adult,
Dependency to independence, penury to affluence?
How can I know where others stand right now, this very moment,
What motivates their acts and fantasies?
All I can do is listen, take their word for it, presume nothing.

The more I live, the more I am alone, inscrutable.
It is a blessing to be one's own man,
Ingest experience like no one else.
And yet, 'tis sad as well.

FRANCINE IS DEAD (1993)

Francine is dead. I heard the news
When last in Paris, knew she died of grief,
Whatever else, remembered vividly
Our last encounter in the sixteenth *arrondissement*,
Ruminating in her slovenly kitchen, bereft
Of any sense of order in her life, ready to die
Even then. The long drive back
From a Versailles *soirée*, the wipers
Clacking inexorably, unfit to cope
With all the rain that overwhelmed
Both wipers and Francine. She was,
As the French say, *au bout*.

Looking back now at the Francine
I knew back in Manhattan in her twenties,
Was it foreseeable that she would come to this?
She was so spunky then, so full of verve, her voice
A warm contralto tinctured with *français*.
She worked for Air France, sharing digs
With a colleague, *vis-à-vis* my flat
On the Westside. She was, as the French say,
Rigolote, all frantic laughter, stuffing pain.

Thirty years, or thereabouts. What took her
From there to here? What indignities
Did life inflict on her, to validate
Her early life perceptions?
I know, but fragments, can but speculate.
A distant father, a mother that told lies
About men and women; a loveless marriage.

What I do know is that Francine
Insisted on a world of her own making,
Denied reality, forced gaiety that grew
More desperate as life assailed her.
She swam against the tide, bravely,
But with premonitions of doom.

FROM THE EDGE OF THE GRAVE (1994)

I reached the nursing home at feeding time,
The wheelchair army rolling down the halls,
Electrified, or with the help of nurses,
Dry spittle gathering in puckered mouths,
A break in endless ennui, eating an event,
Not need. Among the other pallid women
I found my mother, slumped, expressionless,
Her sparse hair gathered in a bow.
Sans any hint of recognition, she sat
Motionless, awaiting nothing, knarled fingers
Working at her hem, folding and unfolding.
I whispered in her ear, stroked her shoulder,
Searching for response. But none came.
I thought of Hamlet's words: "Now get you
To my lady's chamber, and tell her,
Let her paint an inch thick, to this favor she must come."
So must we all, young lovers, golden children,
Kings, politicos, and financiers.
All theory comes to naught, we are no exception,
Our fellow passengers share but one destination.
All we can do is cut our losses, die to fear and greed
Before that last good-bye, count each day our precious last.

AUTUMN REFLECTION (1994)

I meditated open-eyed
Before a rapt autumnal frieze
Of golds, vermilions, rusts, and browns,
A final shoot-the-works.
                        I feared
That in me something too must fail:
The hope that reason might prevail
Before the story ends.
                      How clear
My vision seemed that day, as though
One soul's self-mastery could bring
The world to save itself.
                       But, lo,
The light has faded, boughs are bare
And hope lies barren everywhere.

PAST BOUNDARIES (1994)

Beyond the marsh, traversed by rivulets
The sky hangs low, a Ptolemyan bell
Upon the platter earth.
Faint, distant figures, clustered at bog's edge,
The far horizon scan, breathing surcease
From choking dailiness.

I lean, respiring, on my shepherd's crook,
The marsh grass shifting, swaying in the wind
That cools my face. All apprehension drains,
Silently, into a neat dark puddle, hidden,
Perhaps forever.

It is not I who will emerge
From this vast, open realm, it is not I.
Whoever waits when I return will greet
A strange, transmuted being,
The same in outer form, perhaps, but changed within.

Thus do we pass from landscape to landscape,
From age to age, and those we think we know
Are, but approximations
Of former selves, shifting, like fluid,
From vessel to vessel, shaped
By the eternal potter.

TRANSPORT (1996)

The means of transportation of my life:
The pram our maid let skitter on the pond,
Distracted as she was by some gallant.
The train I took, alone, when I was eight,
To visit grandma in a distant town.
That other train, the boat train from Berlin
That carried me to safety from a place
Of living hell. The ship that took us all
Through sub-infested waters to New York.
The cars, in which I hitchhiked round the West
When I was young and loved the vagrant life.
The boxcar that I lived in and the rig
That took us into town to spend our pay.
The motorbike, on which I tooled around
With girls I picked up at the USO.
The day-trip fishing boat off Montauk Point
Racing to port before a sudden storm.
The third-class sleeping car with open racks
That carried us from Shanghai to Beijing.
The glass-topped tourist boat in Amsterdam,
The steamer down the Rhine, and on the Neva
The windy boat trip through Saint Petersburg.
The flat-boat down the Taracoles River
Amidst the crocodiles, and the canoe
I paddled on the pristine, silent lake
In Williamstown, New York when chores were done.
The raft we rode along the Seti River canyon,
Drenched by the spume as we steered past a whirlpool.
The elephant that took us to the watering hole
Where rhinos brought their young.
The roller-skate escape to Coney Island
From dusty, broiling Brooklyn summer streets.

The thrill of my first motor car, a Beetle,
I did not buy till I was thirty-four.
The helicopter ride 'cross Puget Sound,
Chicago lights seen on a Cessna flight,
Up close and shimmering. The cog-wheel train
That painlessly returned us to the top
Of our five-mile bike run, down, down
Into Kicking Horse Canyon, BC
The Caribbean cruise, in happier days,
On which our in-laws took us, *en famille*.
Horses I rode across the Great Divide
In Colorado's San Juan Wilderness,
And in the North Cascades. The stubborn mule
That so defied me in the Pyrenees
Despite all prodding, and the Frontier plane
That landed, out of fuel, just in time.
The celebration of my first return
To Europe on the Dutch ship *Groote Bear*
Where scores of students shared my birthday cake
And sang the balmy night away with me.
Then, six months later, on the *Ile de France*,
The voyage homeward in the dead of winter.

What voyages are yet to come, I wonder, before
That last, dread voyage 'cross the River Styx?

RENUNCIATION (1997)

We discard what we do not need,
The superficialities of life,
The febrile sunshine friends,
The bombast and the impotent attempts
To thwart the thief of time.
One day these things all come to naught,
The smiles grow weary,
And the vague assurances no longer serve
The purpose of disguising pain,
Of masking pale realities.
Illusions are the last to go.
The certitude that somehow we
Escape the general destiny
Persists into our final years,
And only at the very last
Do we renounce, and are set free.

A POEM FROM DAD (2000)

I sat in silence with my son before his mother's house,
Bathed in the summer warmth. No need to speak;
We understood each other then, had shared our thoughts
And feelings over lunch for nigh two hours,
And now must part.
How dear the moment seemed,
How redolent of trust, as if, having dared much
In conversation, we had sufficient clarity for now
With one another. And though I knew
That in a moment, he would leave the car and go
Into his mother's house, that was all right with me.
I did not feel short-changed, deprived, for by his silence,
His waiting, he had blessed the space I held with him.

PRISONERS ALL (2000)

From the dark corners of the city,
From tenements and drafty shacks and hovels,
From rat-infested basements, trash-strewn alleys
Streams forth a never-ending flow
Of desperate men, shut down, but with bravado
Enveloping them like a protective cloak.

From stately mansions in protected suburbs,
Set 'mid-meticulously tended lawns,
From privileged and richly nourished homes
Streams forth a never-ending flow
Of hollow men, shut down, but with ennui
Enveloping them like a protective cloak.

These streams converge, and as they do,
A fierce, explosive mixture forms,
A social powder keg, resentment, envy,
Fear and greed, the powerless and
Powerful, one lusting to trade places,
The other hanging on for precious life.

VOYAGE (2001)

Our lifetime is a field to be traversed,
A field of vision where, from birth to death,
Our viewing angle changes, day by day.
First, from below, we see life monumental,
O'erwhelming, not to be encompassed.
We rise, circling, as in a spiral,
Inching upward layer by layer,
Kenning the shape of life, its peaks, and hollows,
The skewed effect of light, revealing first,
Then concealing, life seeming random then,
As to a Gulliver in Brobdingnag.

We are now in full flight, a freighted passage
With certain guideposts, yet too few
To calibrate our course. Other trajectories
Cross our own, some in a blur,
Some nearly spent. We sense, intuit
Finitude, the relativity of things, the need
To seize hold of our wheel, to steer
As best we can. But this is hard.
The rudder's not responsive, though we haul
With all our might, cursing the while,
Our compass shows we deviate
From our chosen course, degree by scant degree,
Swerving to latitudes undreamed while yet in port.

At last we find we've reached an alien shore,
An unaccustomed clime, the field
Nearly traversed, and now, after all that,
Strangely dimensioned, smaller than we thought,
Yet not devoid of mystery. The task now
Is to comprehend our journey, the meaning
Of particularities, the currents
We encountered. Were they mere happenstance,
Or self-selected? And is the unknown strand
Where we now find ourselves the one we sought
Unwittingly?
             We have circumnavigated life,
Now have a sense of its harsh limits, yet
Are not ready for our journey's end.
There's more we want to learn, see how
It all ends, all lives, all dreams, all
New attempts to conquer finitude, as if
We did not know the outcome in our hearts.

THE PASSING SCENE (2002)

Sometimes I feel I'm in an alien land,
Surrounded as I am by younger men
Still striving, hunting, gathering.
I contemplate, bemused, the passing scene,
Yes, *passing*, advancing, and receding,
Like flood tide, leaving in its wake
The disappointed dreams of the survivors.

I move through crowds of agitation,
Slower of gait now, breathing more deeply,
Evaluating from a calmer place
What matters more, what less.
I can remember just enough
To resonate with those who seek my counsel,
To lend perspective and to calm their fears.

I've often held myself a long-term optimist
Who sees the world emerging from long sleep,
And am inclined to discount short-term swings
Of markets, moods, and even dire disasters.
Having lived long, I focus on long waves,
Not minor ripples in our history's stream.
I may not live to see nirvana, yet 't will come.

HOMAGE TO ANAGNOS (2002)

I ran into Anagnos in a dream.
How old he looked, how sere and drawn his face.
This manic painter, last seen in his youth
Now had an aspect mad and hollow eyed,
A visage of regrets and mute despair.
He did not recognize me (I was with my wife),
So when I greeted him I saw a look
Of brief confusion, scrolling through
His database of memory.
                            It was
So very long since we were friends,
I'd guess at maybe forty years or so.
Perhaps he had meant more to me than I to him,
Crazed as he was much of the time,
Obsessing about sex with random youth,
Scared of his shadows,
Hallucination hallowed in his art.

How well I still remember them,
Fantastic, spectral canvases that few would buy
(For who would grace his rooms with suicidal rants,
Flights from disaster?)
Yes, Alex would be aged now,
His fires would be banked, and yet, and yet,
His Greek *élan vital* still haunts me,
A Zorba if there ever was one.
Time can't erase the memory of that.

RETURNING TO PORT (2002)

Heureux qui, comme Ulysse, a fait un bon voyage . . .

The trip is done, and oh, the wondrous sights I've seen,
The palaces of Turkestan, sun cresting the hills of Tuscany,
The indolence of peasants dozing in the shade,
Resting from harvesting the orchard fruits,
Succulent melons, peaches barely ripe, and nuts,
The *Seti* river racing through the gorges of Nepal,
Our tiny raft spinning in whirlpools, faces drenched
As we cling to the craft at the abyss,
The sacred *Urubamba* and *Yuana Picchu*,
A festival of earth and spirit framed by peaks
Guarding the ancient Inca city, hidden from the world.

And then the voyages into the human souls
Of those whom I encountered on the way,
The wild-eyed poets, calculating scoundrels,
Sweet lovers and rapacious villains,
The givers, takers, saints, and devils,
And I, who have been all of these
During my voyage through life's seasons.

And now I sail at last, back into port,
Still waiting for me after all these years.
Some buildings have been reconstructed
Beyond all recognition. A generation,
Even two, is gone, but in the children's faces
I still perceive the lineage of those I knew
When young. I tell them of their forbears,
And they listen, respectfully, but barely comprehending
All that went before, the places and the people
That I remember.
                       Never mind. The trip is done,
And now the voyager will stay in port
Until the end.

TURNING CORNERS (2002)

Where are they now that used to be
My intimates? Oh, I recall
That not a day would pass without
At least a phone call, or a sign
Showing that I mattered,
That their lives were intertwined with mine.

And now, perusing an old address book,
I scarce remember who *that* was,
Or *that* one. Yes, the name remains
Faintly familiar, but where is the face
That goes with it?
                     And so I travel
Life's serpentine path, forever turning corners,
Leaving behind, letting slide into oblivion
Those who accompanied me, long ago,
Along that path. Where are they now?
How do they look? How have they *aged?*

I am no longer who I was, and if we met
Today, our greeting would be mere nostalgia.

CURRIED SHRIMP (2004)

The backstreets of Kyoto. Fleeing from the rain,
I duck into a dim-lit noodle bar, sit myself down
And wait for service. I'm alone. The owner yawns
Discreetly in the corner, ambles to his feet.
"*Konnichi wa*"—that's much of what I know
Of Japanese, a language meant to keep the stranger out.
He calls the waitress, reading, looking worn.
"See what he wants," I guess is what he says,
Though I can only guess. I feel like a voyeur,
Eavesdropping on these people, on this culture,
Elusive, to be sensed only through shrines,
Bows, smiles, and circumventions.
They speak no English, he and she, and so I point.
Eventually a steaming dish arrives, curried shrimp
According to the English sign, and, so to speak,
Quite so, given two lone shrimps
Atop the fragrant rice, and yet, a metaphor for all the,
Delicately put, implied communications here.
It's just the culture, not dishonesty, I'm told,
But just a way of putting things, meant to skirt pain.
Better the kindly lie, since losing face won't do.
I eat my rice in silence, focusing my gaze
Downward on my bowl, avoiding eye contact
That is not customary here, then sip my tea,
Ask for my check, and with a murmured *arigato*
Steal back into the darkened, rainy street.

DESPAIR (2005)

What hope is there when the unreas'ning rule,
When all-time-honored wisdom's cast aside
With cold, derisive laughter? Aging dolts
Sit in the seats of power, scoffing
At the cautionary words of those
Who've seen it all before. Cassandra
Hides her face, unheard, unheeded,
Aghast at what's to come.
Is there no succor, are we fated
To endure the unendurable, to drown
In more tsunamis yet undreamed?
Alarming editorials flood the media;
Words, words that no one wants to hear.
We turn the page, switch channels,
Seek divertissements, if only to escape
For precious moments the unwelcome news
Converging from the corners of the world.
We drug ourselves with toys, food, pills,
Most anything to keep the beast at bay.
Tomorrow, yes, we'll face it all tomorrow,
If, that's to say, tomorrow ever comes.

TRACES (2005)

Nothing is lost. The memories, chilled, remain
Unto the utmost reaches of our lives.
Occasions yet undreamed refract their trace,
Though in our consciousness they scarce survive.
The memory of pain untimely borne,
Of hurt inflicted on our tender years,
Parental quarrels, murmurs misconstrued,
The litany of unrequited fears,
A threat'ning bully on a childhood street,
News of bereavement on the telephone,
The darkness of the adolescent soul
When it first senses that we are alone—
Our reason seeks to banish these, the while
They burden our love, inform our gain.
Though times will come when passion's heat subsides,
Still, even then, the memories, chilled, remain.

RETICENCE (February 2007)

These days, when I encounter
Extraordinary men, I know enough
To temper my good vibes with caution,
Rememb'ring disillusionments of old,
Enthusiasms doomed to disappointment.
Expecting little is the better course,
Deferring affirmations pending proof
Of worthiness, lest once again
I find myself confronting feet of clay,
Like mine.

WHAT FATHERS BEAR (2007)

What fathers bear when sons leave
Beggars' description. Empty rooms
Still echo with the voices of the past.
The vacant chair at table, silences
That take the place of sharings
With sons we loved so well, still love,
But now in pain at their departing.
Suddenly we're old, or older at the least.
Suddenly it's only we, without illusions
Of being young with them, playing that game.
Sons' leaving seems like a betrayal,
Their chips now on another number, not ours.
And that embrace which we receive at parting,
A consolation prize, a bittersweet conclusion
To all we shared for oh so many years,
Now past.

THE DARK STAIR (2008)

At the end of that road,
The long, long road through sun-lit valleys
The serpentine road past snow-capped mountains
The road shared with friends and lovers
Yes, that road . . .

At the end of that road
The tranquil road of well-requited longings
The road of vistas and of far horizons
The road that seemed unending
Yes, that road . . .

Now, of a sudden, at the highest peak
That road ends at a precipice
And at the precipice, a dark stair
Leading down, down into impenetrable mist
Marked by a signpost: No way back.

AFTERWARDS (2002)

It is so quiet here. No more cacophony.
Pure spirit reigns in this, the land of peace.
Across the darkened river, through the fog
The flights of corporeal life
Appear frenetic now, a random dance
Leading to nowhere.
As I approached the crossing,
Only then I knew
That comprehension starts
Beyond the earthbound sphere.
And all of you, yet on that distal shore,
Traversing one by one the seasons of your lives,
Age after age, year after year,
Birth, childhood, adolescence,
Prime, decline, and then senescence,
How transient are your joys, your sufferings.
My spirit sends its blessing from afar,
And waits, and waits . . . for your release.

ABOUT THE AUTHOR

Richard Wiener was born in 1927 in the medieval town Wittenberg, the cradle of the Protestant Reformation. As the only Jewish boy in his school, he was subjected to racial persecution, culminating in 1938 in the infamous Night of Broken Glass, the start of the Holocaust. The day his father was taken to the Buchenwald concentration camp, Richard watched as his home was destroyed by Nazi thugs. In 1939, he escaped to England in a child rescue operation, and in 1940 he reached America with his parents.

After service in the U.S. Army, Richard spent many months "on the road", hitchhiking his way around the west. He slept in a box car on the banks of the Yellowstone with a Northern Pacific track gang, worked the night shift at the Anaconda smelter in Montana, and alongside Mexican fruit pickers on a California orchard farm. He was a short order cook in Chicago, a farm laborer in upstate New York, a waiter in Yosemite, a welder and shipping clerk and translator.

After graduation from Columbia College, Richard worked as a staff writer for the American Jewish Committee, and later as an editorial assistant in a technical publishing house. He did graduate work at Princeton, and attended law school at NYU and George Washington University. Despite a lack of technical training, he ended up as an international patent law partner in a small Washington boutique firm. His first novel—*The Aliens*—was a finalist in the Dodd, Mead international fellowship competition, but was not published. A second novel was never completed.

Richard's 20-year marriage ended in divorce in 1990, and produced two children, and, as of this writing, two grandchildren.

In his later years, Richard became involved in personal growth activities, and particularly in the men's movement. He is active in the international organization *The ManKind Project*, as head elder of his Washington center and participant in its transformational weekend trainings. He speaks widely to school and church groups on the subject of forgiveness, and presents a *Power of Forgiveness* workshop at venues around the country.

Since the fall of the Berlin Wall, Richard has returned frequently to the town of his birth, where he has become widely known for his work on reconciliation.

INDEX

A

A burst of shattering glass, 38
A minstrel, fleeing from the rain, and from himself, 12
A night of waiting turns the heart, 19
A single man walks down the empty street, 25
A swan glides in the distance, 26
After all the lamentations, 35
Another hour gone. It's ten past ten, 18
At the end of that road, 68
At the Odeon Casino, 34

B

Beyond the marsh, traversed by rivulets, 50

E

Emerging from the cloistered hall, I paused, 11

F

Falling and falling and falling and falling, 27
Francine is dead. I heard the news, 46
From the dark corners of the city, 55

H

He was a man, recall, only a man, 24
How curious that not till morning light, 33

I

I meditated open-eyed, 49
I ran into Anagnos in a dream, 59
I reached the nursing home at feeding time, 48
I sat in silence with my son before his mother's house, 54
It is so quiet here. No more cacophony, 69

L

Last night you lived, today you are no more, 21

M

Man is constrained to move things, 30
My path is littered with discarded selves, 36

N

Nothing is lost. The memories, chilled, remain, 65

O

Our lifetime is a field to be traversed, 56

R

Rememb'ring the intensity of pain, 66

S

Sometimes I feel I'm in an alien land, 58
So still the land, so still the sea, 14
"Spring's the best time to sell," the agent said, 40

T

The backstreets of Kyoto. Fleeing from the rain, 63
The force goes forward, or it dies, 29
The history of man is more than dates, 44
The means of transportation of my life, 51
The months of my life's spring and summer pass, 23
The New World owes the Old World much, 22
The past revisited: of what avail, 42
The Senator from Maine writes poetry, 28
These days, when I encounter, 66
Tonight you're coming (so, at least, you said), 17
The trip is done, and oh, the wondrous sights Ive seen, 60

W

We discard what we do not need, 53
Whatever I have said or done, 16
What fathers bear when sons leave, 67
What hope is there when the unreas'ning rule, 64
When other lives diverge from mine, 37
Where are they now that used to be, 62
Why be astonished at the change time brings, 43

Y

You are afraid of being an illusion, 15
You bring them back, all the forgotten years, 20